Marriage and Family

The Lutheran Difference Series

Gregory Seltz

CONCORDIA PUBLISHING HOUSE · SAINT LOUIS

Contents

About This Series

"The wedding was beautiful, wasn't it?"

"It certainly was."

"One thing I didn't understand though."

"What's that?"

"In the marriage vows, you Lutherans still say, 'Until death parts us.' Isn't that a little archaic?"

As Lutherans interact with other Christians, they often find themselves struggling to explain their beliefs and practices. Although many Lutherans have learned the "what" of the doctrines of the Church, they do not always have a full scriptural foundation to share the "why." When confronted with different doctrines, they cannot clearly state their faith, much less understand the differences.

Because of insecurities about explaining particular doctrines or practices, some Lutherans may avoid opportunities to share what they have learned from Christ and His Word. The Lutheran Difference Bible study series will identify how Lutherans differ from other Christians and show from the Bible why Lutherans differ. These studies will prepare Lutherans to share their faith and help non-Lutherans understand the Lutheran difference.

Student Introduction

The Bible begins with a marriage (Genesis 1:28; 2:20–24) and ends with a marriage feast (Revelation 19:6–10). Two books of the Bible—Song of Solomon and Ruth—deal extensively with the relationship of husband and wife. In the Old Testament, God is the divine Husband of His bride, Israel. In the New Testament, Christ is the divine Husband of His bride, the new Israel, the Church. The Fourth, Sixth, and Tenth Commandments deal with the relationships created and nurtured by marriage and the family.

While the Bible affirms the value of persons whom God has specially called to a single life, it presumes and is permeated with stories about and instructions for man, woman, and child. It describes the joys and heartaches of husband and wife and the pleasures and the pains of bearing and raising children. The central theme of the Scriptures—a divine Father sends His Son into the world to be born of a virgin mother—is the truth to which every page of Scripture leads.

Yet Christians, at least in the West, seem blind to this biblical emphasis and mute to discussing marriage and the family on the basis of the biblical text. For some, the authority of divine revelation recorded in the Bible and expressed in the created order has been replaced by modern psychology and sociology. Meanwhile, in the public square, the traditional fare of marriage, family, and community has been traded for a mess of individualist pottage.

The Bible and the Lutheran Confessions have a great deal to say about marriage and the family. Luther's insight that marriage is not a sacrament but rather a gift of the created order had profound, positive implications for married life in the Christian West. If marriage and family could be viewed—as Luther viewed them—as God's gifts (and not merely personal rights subject to changing public opinion), society might see a renewed appreciation of marriage and the family.

An Overview of Christian Denominations

The following outline of Christian history will help you understand where the different denominations come from and how they are related to one another. Statements of belief for the different churches are drawn from their official confessional writings.

The Great Schism

Eastern Orthodox: On July 16, 1054, Cardinal Humbert entered the Cathedral of the Holy Wisdom in Constantinople just before the worship service. He stepped to the altar and left a letter condemning Michael Cerularius, patriarch of Constantinople. Cerularius responded by condemning the letter and its authors. In that moment, Christian churches of the East and West were severed from each other. Their disagreements centered on what bread could be used in the Lord's Supper and the addition of the *filioque* statement to the Nicene Creed.

The Reformation

Lutheran: On June 15, 1520, Pope Leo X wrote a letter condemning Dr. Martin Luther for his Ninety-five Theses. Luther's theses had challenged the sale of indulgences, a fund-raising effort to pay for the building of St. Peter's Cathedral in Rome. The letter charged Luther with heresy and threatened to excommunicate him if he did not retract his writings within sixty days. Luther replied by publicly burning the letter. Leo excommunicated him on January 3, 1521, and condemned all who agreed with Luther or supported his cause.

Reformed: In 1522, the preaching of Ulrich Zwingli in Zurich, Switzerland, convinced people to break their traditional Lenten fast. Also, Zwingli preached that priests should be allowed to marry. When local friars challenged these departures from Medieval Church practice, the Zurich Council supported Zwingli and agreed that the Bible should guide Christian doctrine and practice. Churches of the Reformed tradition include Presbyterians and Episcopalians.

Anabaptist: In January 1525, Conrad Grebel, a follower of Ulrich Zwingli, rebaptized Georg Blaurock. Blaurock began rebaptizing others and founded the Swiss Brethren. Their insistence on adult believers' Baptism distinguished them from other churches of the Reformation. Anabaptists attracted social extremists who advocated violence in the cause of Christ, complete pacifism, or communal living. Mennonite, Brethren, and Amish churches descend from this movement.

The Counter Reformation

Roman Catholic: When people call the Medieval Church "Roman Catholic," they make a common historical mistake. Roman Catholicism as we know it emerged after the Reformation. As early as 1518, Luther and other reformers had appealed to the pope and requested a council to settle the issue of indulgences. Their requests were hindered or denied for a variety of theological and political reasons. Finally, on December 13, 1545, thirty-four leaders from the churches who opposed the Reformation gathered at the invitation of Pope Paul III. They began the Council of Trent (1545–63), which established the doctrine and practice of Roman Catholicism.

Post-Reformation Movements

Baptist: In 1608 or 1609, John Smyth, a former pastor of the Church of England, baptized himself by pouring water over his head. He formed a congregation of English Separatists in Holland who opposed the rule of bishops and infant Baptism. This marked the start of the English Baptist churches, which remain divided doctrinally over the theology of John Calvin (Particular Baptists) and Jacob Arminius (General Baptists). In the 1800s, the Restoration Movement of Alexander Campbell, a former Presbyterian minister, adopted many Baptist teachings. These churches include the Disciples of Christ (Christian Churches) and the Churches of Christ.

Wesleyan: In 1729, John and Charles Wesley gathered with three other men to study the Scripture, receive Communion, and discipline one another according to the "method" laid down in the Bible. Later, John Wesley's preaching caused religious revivals in England and America. Methodists, Wesleyans, Nazarenes, and Pentecostals form the Wesleyan family of churches.

Liberal: In 1799, Friedrich Schleiermacher published *Addresses on Religion* in an attempt to make Christianity appealing to people influenced by rationalism. He argued that religion is not a body of doctrines, provable truths, or a system of ethics, but belongs to the realm of feelings. His ideas did not lead to the formation of a new denomination but deeply influenced Christian thinking. Denominations most thoroughly affected by liberalism are the United Church of Christ, Disciples of Christ, and Unitarianism.

Lutheran Facts

All who worship the Holy Trinity and trust in Jesus Christ for the forgiveness of sins are regarded by Lutherans as fellow Christians, despite denominational differences.

Lutheran churches first described themselves as *evangelische* or evangelical churches. Opponents of these churches called them *Lutheran* after Dr. Martin Luther, the sixteenth-century German Church reformer.

Lutherans are not disciples of Dr. Martin Luther but disciples of Jesus Christ. They proudly accept the name *Lutheran* because they agree with Dr. Luther's teaching from the Bible, as summarized in Luther's Small Catechism.

Lutherans believe that God instituted marriage—the lifelong, one-flesh union of husband and wife—in the Garden of Eden when He presented Eve to Adam. Marriage is a First-Article gift (the Creed), having to do with creation. As such, marriage falls under the jurisdiction of the State, not the Church. However, the Church's ministers may conduct weddings on behalf of the State and bless marriages that have already been solemnized before the State.

Lutherans also believe that the estate of marriage is a divine right established by God and cannot be refused or altered either by the State or the Church. Both the State and the Church are obligated to support and encourage marriage. God issued three commandments to specifically protect marriage and the family: the Sixth ("You shall not commit adultery" [Exodus 20:14]), the Tenth ("You shall not covet your neighbor's wife" [v. 17]), and the Fourth ("Honor your father and your mother" [v. 12]).

When and where God wills, married men and women are given the gift of children. Although God never commands the number of children couples should have, the refusal to have children for selfish reasons violates God's command to "be fruitful and multiply" (Genesis 1:28).

Lutherans teach that all earthly authority, including civil authority, flows from the office of parents. God established the family as the basic building block of society.

To prepare for "Foundation in Creation," read Genesis 1:1–2:24.

Foundation in Creation

In the beginning . . .

—Opening of the Book of Genesis

What is marriage? Is marriage merely a civil agreement between two (or possibly more) adults? Is it a relationship based solely on love or sexual attraction? Whatever answers our culture may provide, the Bible says that marriage is much more. Marriage is part of God's design from the beginning to grow and sustain healthy relationships, families, and communities. There's a lot at stake when people say, "I do" and "I will." God instituted marriage in the beginning, and He still guides and blesses it today.

1. How would you define marriage? Why is any discussion of marriage more than just a discussion of the happiness and/or success of one particular couple?

Adam and Eve

Read Genesis 1:20–31.

2. Moses writes that Adam and Eve's (man's) creation was different than that of the animals (contrast Genesis 1:20–25 with 1:26–31). Why is this significant?

3. God placed His stamp of approval on marriage, and indeed all creation, as "very good" (v. 31). Why should we never forget that?

Read Matthew 19:4–6.

4. How does Jesus affirm that God created marriage for one man and one woman for life from the beginning and also for today?

Read Genesis 2:7 and 2:21–22.

5. "Of the dust from the ground" and from "the rib that the LORD God had taken from the man" are important truths for understanding God's sanctified view of physical life. Why?

6. How does the Bible's view of marriage differ from other views of marriage, old and new?

Read Genesis 1:28.

7. How was the marriage of Adam and Eve to bless not only them, but also all of God's creation?

God's Design

8. In Genesis 1 and 2, the Bible teaches God's design for human relationships. Even though sin mars the beautiful gift of marriage, why is it very important to guard and teach marriage as the foundational human relationship? (Keep in mind that there are biblically legitimate reasons for people to live chaste single lives as well.)

9. List some positive benefits healthy marriages bring to individuals and to society at large.

Extended Blessings

Marriage is a relationship rooted in creation, part of God's plan for the human family. The institution of marriage "from the beginning" is intended not only to bless men, women and children, but also all of creation. Fidelity toward marriage's foundational purpose undergirds a healthy sense of human intimacy, sexuality, partnership, family and through the family, a healthy community.

10. Knowing God's will about marriage, what can you do to encourage such a positive understanding among your friends and neighbors?

11. Marriage is also foundational to community life in general. Why is it important to resist teachings that merely reduce marriage's benefits to the happiness of the couple alone? Why is marriage, even among non-Christians, much more than that?

12. How then are all issues of sexual immorality, including sexual activity outside of the one-flesh union of husband and wife, truly actions that shake peoples' foundations? Why then are they not to be trifled with?

For Reflection

When a man and a woman wed, they enter upon a relationship which in its origin and attendant blessings bears the stamp of divine approval. God, having created His living, breathing masterpiece, the first man, laid down this universal truth for all subsequent ages: "It is not good that the man should be alone" (Genesis 2:18); that is, it is not compatible with his highest happiness, his complete usefulness, to remain unmarried. This declaration of divine wisdom was then translated into divine action; God created for man a helpmate who corresponded to him physically, mentally, and spiritually. And when the first bride in all history was presented to the first groom, "the voice that breathed o'er Eden that earliest wedding-day" pronounced its primal blessing. This divine benediction, the majestic "And God blessed them," has become the sacred pledge of happiness in Christian marriage.

Walter A. Maier, *For Better Not for Worse* (Concordia Publishing House, 1939), p. 17.

Point to Remember

We will exult and rejoice in you; we will extol your love more than wine. Song of Solomon 1:4

To prepare for "Unique and Distinct," review Genesis 2:15–23.

Unique and Distinct

Viva le difference!

—French saying

Are men truly from Mars and women truly from Venus? No, men and women are human beings from the planet earth! While the diversity and gifts of male and female are often misunderstood, it wasn't always so. God's plan for human beings and all His creation was for its beauty and wonder, its harmony in diversity. Men and women have always been unique and distinct, but such distinctions are intended as opportunities for love and service toward each other, not for misunderstanding and domination.

13. People often think that love is the fullest on a couple's wedding day. Why is this not completely true? What happens when one forgets the difference between our love for each other and Christ's love for others through us?

Male and Female

Read Genesis 1:27 and 2:15–23.

14. Genesis 1:27 states that God created male and female in His image. How does this truth support the equality of men and women and yet still maintain their uniqueness?

15. "Bone of my bones and flesh of my flesh" (2:23) tells of the intimacy between Adam and Eve. Why do anti-female and anti-male

views of this relationship pale in comparison to the Bible's view of men and women being created for each other?

16. "It is not good that the man should be alone" (2:18) was God's declaration that His creative process for humanity was not finished with Adam. What hints does this provide for us concerning marriage's purpose in God's creative plan for humanity?

17. When God defines Eve's relationship to Adam as a helper or partner, and when Adam sees Eve as part of himself, how does this help us to view gender identity as an opportunity to serve the opposite sex?

Self-discovery

18. People sometimes seek therapy to find themselves. Why is marriage still one of the best places for men and women to find out who they are, especially from God's viewpoint?

19. From your point of view, what was lost from Adam and Eve's relationship in Genesis 3? How did that change things?

20. In spite of the reality of sin, can you envision a healthy relationship where husband and wife are truly different yet one? If

compatibility is not the ultimate issue, what is (for help, see Genesis 2; 2 Corinthians 4; 5:17–20)?

Natural Love

Marriage's relational nature reflects but does not mirror exactly the harmony of God within Himself as three divine persons (one aspect of man being created in God's image). Sin not only destroyed that harmony between persons, but also set male and female against each other. Marriages that are blessed by Jesus Christ are not only blessed to be happy, but are also blessed to reclaim that love and harmony that was once before so natural.

21. In John 16:13–15 and 10:29–30, the Bible speaks about the relationship of the trinitarian persons: Father, Son, and Holy Spirit. How is this reflected in the plurality, diversity, and harmony of the male-female relationship in Genesis 2?

22. How does sin often cloud the positive nature of male and female differences? What are some ways that Christians can reaffirm them?

23. How is the Bible's understanding of finding oneself in service to others challenged by the uniqueness of and differences between men and women?

For Reflection

Christ's endorsement of matrimony is supported throughout the Scriptures. When the prophets of the Old Covenant sought to impress upon their own countrymen the magnificence of Jehovah's grace to Israel and the mystic union that bound Him to His people, they could find no more fitting symbol than marriage, the intimate union that exists between husband and wife. Long into the New Testament the same exaltation of marriage continues. Writing to the Ephesians (5:25) and consciously speaking of a great mystery, St. Paul compares the love which a husband bears for his wife to that self-effacing devotion with which Jesus loved the Church. And as the light of revelation illumines the closing pages of St. John's Apocalypse, the bride, the holy Church, gazes along the horizon of prophecy for the coming of the Bridegroom, Christ.

Walter A. Maier, *For Better Not for Worse* (Concordia Publishing House, 1939), p. 75.

Point to Remember

As a lily among brambles, so is my darling among the young women. Song of Solomon 2:2

To prepare for "Biblical Intimacy," read Genesis 2:24–25 and Matthew 19:4–6.

Biblical Intimacy

Love conquers all.

—Virgil

The most precious words that a person can hear are "I love you." The most precious actions a person can see are those that concretely demonstrate "I love you." But love is not merely an emotion. It is a commitment of the will to do for the other person what God says is best. Love is even the willingness to put emotion aside for the sake of another. A love that grows from such a commitment allows space for emotional, physical, and personal intimacy to grow. When a person says, "I will" or "I do," the opportunity for real intimacy begins.

24. People say that the Bible is prudish about intimacy, especially sexual intimacy. Why is this caricature incorrect (see the Song of Solomon; 1 Corinthians 6:18–20; 7:3–5)? How would you characterize the Bible's view of intimacy?

Leave and Hold Fast

Read Genesis 2:24–25.

25. Describe the picture of intimacy that the Bible paints in the marital relationship. Comment on the realistic view that is presented in these two verses.

26. How do "leave" and "hold fast" speak of the activity that builds intimacy in marriage from God's creative intentions? Who builds the oneness?

27. How do "leave" and "hold fast" relate to the marriage vows, the "I dos"?

Read Matthew 19:4–6.

28. Jesus reiterates that male and female were created for each other. How does His warning against anyone separating such a union speak of the depth of marital intimacy?

Read 1 Corinthians 7:1–7.

29. Why are Paul's instructions concerning marriage both down to earth and intensely spiritual?

30. In Genesis, marriage creates the opportunity for physical and spiritual intimacy. In 1 Corinthians 7, marriage helps remedy sinful desire. How are both true today and why?

Loving Commitment

31. The Bible teaches that intimacy flows from commitment; it does not precede it. Why does living together actually undermine a couple's potential for intimacy?

32. If you are or have been married, when you look back, when were the times that it was most difficult to stay focused (to leave and

hold fast) on your spouse? Why? What prevented you from finding a way to love your spouse? What would you do differently today?

Commitment Comes First

Biblical intimacy is born of a commitment to learn how to love another as he or she needs to be loved. Intimacy is a gift that flows from two actions of one's will: leaving and holding fast. Such a commitment is to be lifelong. Marriage is that God-ordained relationship of commitment, fidelity, and service that gives a man and a woman the opportunity and the space for such intimacy to grow.

33. Why is romance such an important part of a healthy marriage?

34. The Bible says that sexual sins are especially harmful because they are sins a person commits "against his own body" (1 Corinthians 6:18). How might this also apply to the embodied oneness of husband and wife?

For Reflection

Because marriage comes from God above and not from man or beast below, it involves moral, not merely physical, problems. A sin against the commandment of purity is a sin against God, not simply the outraging of convention, the thoughtlessness of youth, the evidence of bad taste. The Savior tells us that, when God's children are joined in wedlock, they are united by Him, and beneath the evident strength and love that this divine direction promises is an ominous warning. Those who tamper with God's institution have lighted the fuse to the explosive of retributive justice. Marriage is so holy that of all social sins its violation invokes the most appalling consequences. . . . Throughout history red warnings mark the final record of devastated nations that forgot the divine origin of marriage and its holiness.

Walter A. Maier, *For Better Not for Worse* (Concordia Publishing House, 1939), pp. 76–77.

Point to Remember

My beloved is mine, and I am his. Song of Solomon 2:16

To prepare for "Exercising Faith and Love," read Ephesians 5:15–33 and 1 Peter 3:1–9.

Exercising Faith and Love

What God has joined together, let no one put asunder.

—From the marriage rite (*Lutheran Worship Agenda*)

It has been said that in marriage the husband is the head and the wife is the heart. Paul also uses biological terms when he refers to the husband as the head and the wife as the body. Just as no human being could survive with only a head (absent a body) or only a body (without a head), no marriage can survive without the healthy participation and mutual support of both husband and wife.

35. Our culture may be beginning to realize that the complementary qualities of men and women are good. List the unique blessings that a man and a woman each bring to marriage. How might such differences provide an opportunity to love?

Mutual Submission, Submission, and Love

Read Ephesians 5:15–21.

36. Put v. 21 into your own words. Why is it important to remember that this passage concerns the mutual submission that all believers offer to one another through the work of the Holy Spirit (see Galatians 3:26–29)?

37. How does this passage direct us to the biblical focus of loving Christian service to others? In thinking about marriage, is marriage merely an exercise of love, or is it also an exercise of faith? Explain.

38. Who is the source of sustaining power for both healthy gender roles and healthy marriages (see 1 Corinthians 11:11–12)?

Read Ephesians 5:22–33.
39. Note how the wife is to "submit" to her husband (vv. 22–24) and how the husband is to "love" his wife in a wholly self-sacrificial way (vv. 25–30). How are their actions toward each other different but complementary?

40. What does the Bible mean when it discusses headship (see Matthew 20:25–28; Ephesians 5:25, 28; 1 John 3:16, 18)? How does self-sacrificial love provide insight as to what the husband's headship entails?

41. The man is the head and the wife is the body in the marriage relationship (see Genesis 2:18–23; Proverbs 31:10–31). How might this affect a woman's view of her role in marriage?

Read 1 Peter 3:1–9.
42. In this passage, Peter demonstrates how the complementary duties of husband and wife toward each other are supportive and affirming. How does the phrase "heirs with you of the grace of life" help define the ultimate purpose of marriage lived out in God's grace?

Love in Action

43. The Bible teaches that husbands and wives should serve each other in faith and love because each is unique (and needing forgiveness as well). How might your view of love in action change once you realize that even a "perfect" spouse would still need to be loved in a unique way? How does this actually make marriage a lifelong opportunity of discovery?

44. Is the word *submission* a word of strength or weakness? Explain your answer. Discuss some concrete, positive ways that your answer might be applied to relationships and responsibilities outside of marriage.

Learning to Love

People say that compatibility is the key to a relationship. While surely helpful, the Bible actually speaks about love as the commitment to serve a person unique and distinct from you. Service toward one's spouse is not merely an act of love, but also an exercise of faith in the Christ who fearfully and wonderfully created man as "male and female" for each other (Genesis 1; Matthew 19:5–6). Through faith in our Savior, husband and wife are enabled to practice His forgiving love in marriage.

45. Explain how the mutual submission (Ephesians 5:21) of all believers out of reverence for Christ is a prelude to the self-sacrificial love husbands owe their wives, and the submission wives owe their husbands. In what sense has Christ reclaimed the relationship that Adam and Eve shared in the garden prior to their sin?

46. A man learns to be a man especially by serving his wife in a self-sacrificial way. A woman learns to be a woman especially by submitting to the service of such a man. Discuss.

For Reflection

When at Calvary, all history's holy of holies, we pause to survey the extent of Christ's devotion to the Church, we bow before a love that came to give rather than to take, to serve instead of being served, a love that loved until the end, that bitter end when, in the greatest sacrifice of which even divine mercy could conceive, Christ died that His Church might live. By the impulse of this divine love the discussion of the term "obey" becomes more academic than actual in any truly Christian marriage. Glorifying Christ, the husband will be impelled to cherish his wife with an intense affection, to acknowledge her virtues and accomplishments, to minimize her frailties, to perform the many services of love by working for her, providing for her, living for her, and, if necessary, even dying for her, as Christ gave Himself for the Church.

Walter A. Maier, *For Better Not for Worse* (Concordia Publishing House, 1939), pp. 464–65.

Point to Remember

Eat, friends, drink, and be drunk with love. Song of Solomon 5:1

To prepare for "More than Romance," read Ephesians 5:31–32; 1 Corinthians 13:1–13; and Romans 12:1–2, 9–21.

More than Romance

Love is blind.

—Jessica in Shakespeare's *The Merchant of Venice*

Marriage isn't merely romance? Impossible! Whoever heard of such a thing! Properly speaking, marriage is about love: the joyful, heartfelt, persevering, committed, "willing to learn" love practiced by folks who can't wait to see what this is all about. Romance may kindle and rekindle that flame, but only love sustains it.

47. Dietrich Bonhoeffer noted that marriage isn't merely a personal issue; it is an office. Marriage cannot be reduced to the love that one has for another. Rather, the opposite is true. Marriage sustains the love experienced and expressed in marriage. Is Bonhoeffer correct?

Christ and His Bride

Read Ephesians 5:31–32.

48. Notice in these verses how Paul compares the relationship of husband and wife to Christ and the Church. What are the similarities? What are the differences?

Read 1 Corinthians 13:1–13; John 15:12–13; and Ecclesiastes 4:7–12.

49. These passages talk about God's love. What kind of love is that?

27

50. How does God's love enable and sustain a couple's marriage? Why does one miss the point if one reads these passages merely as examples for us to follow in how to love each other?

Read Romans 12:1–2; 1 Corinthians 7:3–5; and Colossians 3:12–17.

51. Practically speaking, what is the role of worship, Bible study, and prayer in a healthy marriage (see Romans 12:1–2; 1 Corinthians 7:3–5)?

52. In 1 Corinthians 7, how does Paul demonstrate the priority of prayer—even the prayers one makes for his or her spouse? Why does this elevate both and not diminish either?

53. Notice how Colossians 3:12–17 precedes Paul's exhortation of one's duties to others in one's family. What does this teach about the source of love in marriage and about the marriage relationship as an arena of practiced grace?

The Power of Forgiveness

54. The Bible understands not only the different needs of men and women as they relate to each other, but also the reality of sin and selfishness in marriage. Why, then, is God's forgiveness in Christ the underlying strength for Christian marriage (see Ephesians 4:31–32)?

Can you apply your Baptism, Absolution, the Gospel, and the Lord's Supper to your marriage relationship?

55. Thinking of your premarital plans, did you dwell much on faith issues? worship issues? Knowing what you know now, how are those things the most important of all, especially in and for marriage? Why?

His Love Is Our Strength

Jesus calls us to love as He has loved and continues to love us. That exhortation is never more real than in the marriage relationship. Christ doesn't merely call us to follow His example. Rather, He beckons us to draw on His forgiving grace and love. His forgiving grace received in the means of grace enables husbands and wives to put His love into practice.

56. Explain how romance may ignite people's love for each other but only God's love can truly sustain a healthy relationship.

57. How is God's grace in Christ the only solid source of power to live life serving one's spouse? Why is this selfless esteem more powerful than the self-esteem relationships for which our world clamors?

For Reflection

The avalanche of domestic misunderstanding that starts insignificantly from some small, selfish act and soon assumes devastating proportions can be averted only by the sincerity of resolution which renews Joshua's promise of old, "As for me and my house, we will serve the Lord" (Joshua 24:15). A home built on this resolution may be shaken by the storms of unemployment, illness, suffering, and death; but it will have a peace which a self-indulgent world knows not, for it will have Christ.

Walter A. Maier, *For Better Not for Worse* (Concordia Publishing House, 1939), p. 545.

Point to Remember

Set me as a seal upon your heart, as a seal upon your arm; for love is strong as death, jealousy is fierce as the grave. Song of Solomon 8:6

To prepare for "Leaving a Legacy," read the Fourth Commandment; 1 Peter 2:13–17; Ephesians 6:1–4; Deuteronomy 6:1–9; and Proverbs 22:6.

Leaving a Legacy

Many children, many cares; no children, no felicity.

—Christian Nestell Bovee

In God's plan, families don't exist for their happiness alone. Families are the place where father, mother, and children receive and share Christ's forgiveness with each other. In the family, each member learns to live with each other on His terms. Through the family, generations of children and grandchildren come to know that the Father's love in Jesus Christ, by the power of His Holy Spirit, makes all this possible. Families and family members not only bless each other, they also are the foundation for a wider community and a civilized society.

58. What is a family worth today? What special value are godly families to the communities in which they live and serve?

Doing Your Duty

Read Deuteronomy 6:1–9; Proverbs 22:6; Matthew 23:37; and Hebrews 12:6–10.

59. According to Deuteronomy, what does the Bible say are vital duties of parents, especially fathers?

60. How does Proverbs 22:6 express the purpose of godly parenting?

61. Matthew 23:37 and Hebrews 12:6–10 give us some clues as to the different kinds of love that mothers and fathers bring to parenting. Why is parenting more than just doing what comes naturally (see also Titus 2:1–5)?

Read Ephesians 6:1–4.

62. Children are God's blessing to father and mother (Matthew 19:13–14). How and why? What wisdom and blessing does God wish to teach through faithful parenting?

63. How does abortion not only deny the enormous value of a child, but also ultimately undermine one of the purposes of marriage?

Read the Fourth Commandment and 1 Peter 2:13–17.

64. God ordains all earthly authorities for our good. How is the home the place where children first learn how to respect order and authority?

65. Explain how adultery, serial divorce, or abusive or faithless parenting disrupts not only families, but also affects the wider community.

66. How does governmental authority relate to the authority of parents? How does this begin to lay a foundation for the proper roles of the Church and the State in our lives?

Mother and Father

67. Why are households with two opposite-sex parents important? Why are they a special blessing to children?

68. Today, some who are born into Christian homes, study, work, and recreate almost exclusively among people of faith, with virtually no contact with non-Christians. Is this God's purpose for the family? Why or why not?

Community Blessing

The family is foremost that place where the promises of Jesus Christ, the truths of God's Word, are practiced for restoration, redemption, and love. The Church, as God's extended family of faith, exists to gather families to encourage and strengthen them for their work. Such work extends out from godly families to the communities in which they live. Civic authorities exist in God's plan to provide peace and stability for the Church and the family to do their work. The Church and the home are fundamental not only in God's plan of salvation, but also in the plan of practicing that salvation for the whole world to see.

69. Children are a common blessing in marriage through which husband and wife must decide together how to love and discipline.

How does working out such things help prepare one for work in society as well?

70. The Bible teaches that the family unit is the foundation of society. Why is it important to remember that while the government may help in certain family issues, it can never replace the value and work of mothers and fathers for their children?

For Reflection

With the additional emphasis that the Word of God lays upon the individual in eternity, the names of the elect recorded in the Book of Life, the acknowledgment of each faithful believer by the Savior Himself before His Father in heaven, Dives beholding Abraham and Lazarus in his bosom, no doubt remains in the Christian's mind. He believes that, when the New Testament speaks of "the whole family in heaven" (Ephesians 3:15), it includes in this vast picture of the ten thousand times ten thousand the recognition of those who were united in the Spirit-blessed family here on earth.

Walter A. Maier, *For Better Not for Worse* (Concordia Publishing House, 1939), p. 560.

Point to Remember

So Boaz took Ruth, and she became his wife. And he went in to her, and the LORD gave her conception, and she bore a son. . . . They named him Obed. He was the father of Jesse, the father of David. Ruth 4:13, 17

Leader Guide

This guide is provided as a "safety net," a place to turn for help in answering questions and enriching discussion. It will not answer every question raised in your class. Please read it, along with the questions, before class. Consult it in class only after exploring the Bible references and discussing what they teach. Please note the different ability levels of your class members. Some will easily find the Bible passages listed in this study; others will struggle. To make participation easier, team up members of the class. For example, if a question asks you to look up several passages, assign one passage to one group, the second to another, and so on. Divide the work! Let participants present the answers they discover.

Each topic is divided into four easy-to-use sections.

Focus introduces key concepts that will be discovered.

Inform guides the participants into Scripture to uncover truths concerning a doctrine.

Connect enables participants to apply what is learned in Scripture to their lives and provides them an opportunity to formulate and articulate a defense of a key doctrine.

Vision provides participants with practical suggestions for extending the theme of the lesson out of the classroom and into the world.

Foundation in Creation

Objectives

By the power of the Holy Spirit working through God's Word, participants will (1) learn that marriage is an institution created and ordained by God and woven into the very fabric of creation from the beginning; (2) affirm that while sin has marred this institution, fidelity in the marriage of one man to one woman for life is still something to strive for; and (3) ponder that though marriage is also a civil estate for Christian and non-Christian the Christian marriage is sanctified through faith in Christ.

Opening Worship

Sing "Praise God, from Whom All Blessings Flow" (*LW* 461). The connection is self-explanatory but necessary. A true appreciation of marriage is first to see it as it is, a blessing from God for the world in which we live. It is a source of joy, blessing, and even peace for society. Open with prayer.

Focus

Ask someone to read the opening paragraph out loud. Ask participants to comment on the discussion-starter question.

1. Answers will vary. Impress upon participants the depth of marriage's purpose and blessing, not just its personal benefit to a particular couple. Remember, most people tend to see these things only from the viewpoint of their own experience. Try to prepare them for the fuller discussion of the Word of God concerning marriage and the family, even as you affirm that such truths will be a blessing to them as well.

Adam and Eve (Inform)

2. In Genesis 1, animals are said to come from the earth (see Genesis 1:24, "Let the earth bring forth living creatures according to

their kinds"). Of course their life also consists in the creative Word of God that calls them forth, but in a different way than man. Man's relationship to his Creator is much more intimate. In Genesis 1:26, God says, "Let Us make man in Our image." God's investment in man as the crown of His creation is seen both in God's more direct participation in this part of His creation and in the unique status that man has reflecting God to creation in original righteousness (Genesis 1:27; Apology of the Augsburg Confession II 9, 15–22). Male and female may be creatures of the earth, but they are creatures unlike any other. This biblical truth is foundational to all discussions about personal human identity, intimacy, and gender issues, as well as personal responsibility and accountability toward other people and God's creation in general.

3. The marital relationship was part of God's plan for men and women from the beginning (see Apology of the Augsburg Confession XIII 14). It is important to remember that God deemed marriage "very good," namely, that marriage is a normative relationship for human beings in creation. Men and women were meant to be together, reflecting God's goodness, righteousness, and love, not only in their service to each other, but in their mutual service to all creation. While God exempts some from marriage by nature, incapacity, or through the spiritual gift of chastity (see Matthew 19:11–12; 1 Corinthians 7:7–8; Apology XXIII 16–22), marriage remains foundational this side of heaven (see Matthew 22:30; Apology XXIII 7–13).

4. Jesus Himself reiterates God's intent for marriage by claiming the original, creative plan of marriage as normative. True, sin challenges God's original plan for marriage; some resist marriage because it binds them to another, while others attempt (and, sadly, succeed) in redefining marriage according to their own terms. This they do against God's Word recorded in the Bible and the creative Word still present and active (and observable!) in creation. But, even now, marriage is to be striven for, sought out as a blessing from God.

5. "Of dust from the ground" (Genesis 2:7) and "the rib . . . taken from the man" (2:22) root any discussion about the spiritual nature of human relationships where it belongs: in the physical realm of life. In God's plan for humanity, marriage is a spiritual-physical relationship lived to its fullest in the world. In the Christian worldview, there is neither a loathing of the physical nor an unhealthy focus on it alone. Rather, spiritual and physical life for men and women, especially in marriage, is part of God's plan. This applies not only to the hopes and

dreams of the couple on their wedding day, but also to the fullness of their lives and their children's lives and for the blessing of the communities in which they live.

6. There are many religious and philosophical traditions that claim the physical or material areas of life are unimportant or even evil. Such was the case among the Gnostics and the Manichaeans. That's not the case in Christianity. While the Bible proclaims the depth of the reality of sin and evil, it also proclaims the original goodness of creation and God's redemptive action in the fully divine and fully human Christ not just for the soul, but for the whole person: body *and* soul. Creation, Christ's incarnation, crucifixion, and bodily resurrection, the resurrection of all the dead on the Last Day, and the gifts of the Sacraments serve as examples of how God's love is expressed and enjoyed in the flesh. Contemporary views of marriage that focus on the disembodied rights of individuals apart from their created gender differences, or children manufactured in labs apart from real human relationships found in families, eerily reflect those ancient heresies.

7. It is important to remember marriage's purposes: the intimate love and mutual support of man and wife, the procreation of children (the building of a family of such love), and the restraining of sexual sins (Genesis 1:27–28; 1 Corinthians 7:2; Apology of the Augsburg Confession XXIII 7–17). Genesis 1:28 tells us that God wished for His whole creation to experience that loving leadership in action. *Rule* is a word for service in the Bible. Romans 15:12 tells us that Jesus' rule will be a cause for hope. So also is the family of humanity (male, female, and offspring) to be a blessing to the rest of God's creation as faithful stewards of what God has put under their direction.

God's Design (Connect)

8. While God gives His human creatures a variety of relationships in which to exercise our vocations of loving service (mother, uncle, teacher, electrician, student, voter), only marriage encompasses full bodily and spiritual intimacy as designed by the Creator. Also, no other human relationship has been endowed by the Father with the natural capacity for procreation: extending through children the gift of life.

9. A healthy marriage extends itself into and influences positively healthy relationships between parents and children. Children who witness parents modeling appropriate behaviors—loving care and

service—pattern their behavior and extend it to others. A home filled with love, proper attention and care, and loving discipline when needed is the basis not only for good children, but good citizens as well. Stable homes promote stable children, who in turn become stable adults and productive workers, managers, caretakers, nurses, citizens, and so on.

Extended Blessings (Vision)

10. Answers may vary. Whether one is married, has been married, or will never marry, marriage as an institution exists for all. A positive view of marriage calls men and women to direct their love away from themselves toward each other, their families, and ultimately their communities. Practicing such love helps us all become more mature in our care for each other, sensing more clearly what is important in life.

11. Selfish love is the antithesis to God's love (1 Corinthians 13). Selfish rule is the antithesis to God's servant rule (Psalm 145:15–16; Matthew 20:28). Marriage as an institution is not only to foster healthy, loving relationships, but it is to curb unhealthy ones as well (1 Corinthians 7:9–11). Even those who do not seek the triune God's blessing for their marriage realize the value of strong marriages and families to the communities in which they live. Companionship, intimacy, partnership, and family are needs that human beings understand *by nature* to be sustained in and by marriage (Romans 2:14–15; Apology of the Augsburg Confession XXIII 8–13).

12. First and foremost, sexual immorality of any sort challenges the authority of the Genesis account and Christ's reiteration of it in Matthew 19. Male and female were created in God's image for each other, for mutual love and companionship, and for the purposes of family and the building of healthy community. All immoral lifestyles that debase the commitment that undergirds marriage not only shake society, they begin to destroy the opportunity for healthy love and intimacy between men and women too. Leviticus 18 delineates who can and cannot marry, but the need for such prohibitions also demonstrates how quickly society can unravel into unhealthy, destructive behaviors once the sanctity of marriage and the family has been destroyed (see Romans 1:18–32). As such, this is a warning and an invitation for all to "let the marriage bed be undefiled" (Hebrews 13:4).

Unique and Distinct

Objectives

By the power of the Holy Spirit working through God's Word, participants will (1) learn the Bible's view of male and female made in the image of God, (2) appreciate that God's creative intent for men and women as true partners before Him is the only antidote for anti-female or anti-male views, and (3) give thanks for the uniqueness and differentiation between male and female as opportunities for love and service.

Opening Worship

Sing "Our Father, by Whose Name" (*LW* 465). All three verses reiterate the centrality of God's love in the purposes of marriage. Just as God's love is needed, so also His direction and teaching concerning what male and female are to be in relationship to Him and to each other. Open with prayer.

Focus

Ask someone to read the opening paragraph out loud. Ask participants to comment on the discussion-starter question.

13. Our love for each other ebbs and flows. It often responds positively when emotional and physical needs are met. But such love does not often sustain a marriage. God's love in Christ (1 Corinthians 13) is the kind of love that cares for the unlovable. It seeks to love. It loves not only the friend, but also the enemy (see Romans 5:6–8). Such love can begin to recapture the "from the beginning" essence of marriage that was lost in man's rebellion against God.

Male and Female (Inform)

14. Genesis 1 says that God created male and female in His image, clearly affirming their equality and mutual worth in God's eyes. The Bible's view of male and female is that of intrinsic value. All

discussions of the uniqueness of roles, gifts, or abilities must start with this basic biblical principle. Genesis 2:22–23 and Ephesians 5:28 also express the biblical view of the mutually high intrinsic value of both male and female as creatures of God. Any discussion about the biblical view of male and female must deal with their uniqueness with respect to each other and their equality before their Creator.

15. The Bible clearly teaches that men and women were created for each other. Their uniqueness and differentiation is clearly for the sake of the other and not merely for their individuality. Male and female may be unique, but such uniqueness was never meant for isolation. One can't truly appreciate the biblical fullness of what it means to be a man or woman outside the activity of serving another. Marriage is the foundational relationship where this can happen.

Adam's declaration of joy concerning Eve is telling. Though Eve was surely different, her intimacy with Adam as well as Adam's with her is proclaimed in Adam's recognition both of Eve's uniqueness, "bone" and "flesh," and of their physical/emotion connection, "of my bones" and "of my flesh." Each reflected the other. Each was fully human individually and yet was also made to be the spiritual, physical, and emotional partner to the other as part of God's plan. Anti-female or anti-male views of this relationship are based on power and the desire for control. These power plays are not based on the reality of God's call for men and women to be servants to one another as part of God's creation, nor in His purpose for marriage in the redemptive power and example of Jesus.

16. Genesis 1 and 2 speak about human beings before their fall into sin. Adam was perfect but alone. When God speaks of man's being alone as "not good," it directs humanity toward God's finalized creative purpose in male-female relationships: marriage. God's plan was that men and women would look toward each other in loving service. In fact, it's important to note in Genesis 2:22 that God "brought her to the man." She was God's gift, an opportunity for Adam to learn not only about himself, but also about God's love and care for him through her. God's resources of life, love, joy, peace, and so on were meant to be shared. Adam without Eve is unfinished business from God's point of view. The original intent for men and women was to find their joy in each other as they not only served the other's needs but also as they reflected God's glory and honor in their stewardship over God's creation.

17. Genesis 2 demonstrates an order in creation. Adam is created out of the dust of the ground and Eve out of Adam. The relationship between husband and wife is not merely a negotiated contractual agreement but rather a created reality in which men and women learn to serve each other as God intended them to serve. In such service to the other, the Bible shows that a healthy identity of male and female is to be found. Such an understanding of the created unity and diversity of men and women is the key to the biblical intimacy (the one-flesh union) that is built into marriages that honor such teaching.

Self-discovery (Connect)

18. Adam cries out that this is "bone of my bones and flesh of my flesh" (Genesis 2:23). Adam sees that Eve is unlike any other of God's good creation (2:19–20). This is what Adam also learned about himself as he saw Eve, the one whom God had given him to love. Eve, in her partnership with Adam, also demonstrated the fullness of her God-given identity as Adam's helpmate.

19. Sin corrupted the harmony that existed in the diversity and uniqueness of Adam and Eve. Genesis 3:12–13 shows a radically changed relationship where both turn on each other and begin to protect themselves. Their uniqueness in status and service to each other now, in the absence of self-sacrificing love, becomes a means for suspicion. Sexuality and intimacy are also now prone to be used as weapons against each other.

20. The New Testament speaks very matter-of-factly of marriage as a place for mutual love and intimacy (Ephesians 5:19–31), an institution to protect against immorality (1 Corinthians 7:2–5), and as an institution that can be reclaimed in the forgiveness of Jesus Christ (1 Corinthians 6:12–20). In Genesis, Eve was naturally for Adam and Adam for Eve. In the New Testament, our bodies are reclaimed for such service by God's redemptive love in Jesus poured into our lives through Baptism. Our bodies now can be "offered" again in His love to one another (see Romans 6:4–14 and 12:1–5). The New Testament calls us to reclaim the original intention of the Creator in our marriages, daily reconciled to God and each other, as we receive and share God's love as His "jars of clay" (2 Corinthians 4:7).

Natural Love (Vision)

21. There is a diversity of person in God even as He is one in nature, or essence. There is a mutual recognition of the uniqueness of the Father, the Son, and the Spirit, yet a oneness in essence, will, love, and purpose. There is a submission of the Spirit to the Son and the Son to Father, even as the Father relates to His creation in redemptive mercy. These realities in God's nature are reflected in the love that men and women have been created to share with each other as they learn to honor and celebrate their unique callings toward each other.

22. Sin turns the unique honor of and specific service that men and women render to each other into competition, man against woman and woman against man. Christians can begin to affirm the unique blessings of men and women according to the Bible, honoring such things because God has called us toward such a view of male and female. Such picturing of men and women according to their scriptural potential (in the reality of real forgiveness and mercy through Christ's death and resurrection) actually enables people to become the men or women God created them to be. Solicit examples from participants.

23. We are taught today that marriages, indeed all relationships, succeed based on compatibility. The Bible's view of marriage is that it is the commitment to learn to love that sustains marriage and not merely a compatibility of interests and talents. In fact, learning to love that which is *not* like you is the core capability and capacity of God's love in Jesus Christ.

In the Bible, *porneia* (Romans 7:2) concerns all sexual sins outside of marriage. Each sex was created for the other. Heterosexual immorality uses the opposite sex merely as an object to fulfill its desire. Homosexuality is the ultimate form of self-love: it rejects the biblical proclamation that man and woman were created for each other and that there is a profound oneness and healthy identity in service to the opposite sex. It may be true that on one level men understand men better and women understand women better. However, each are to grow in their understanding of male and female from God's point of view to learn to love that which is different from ourselves and to reflect God's love for us to others.

Biblical Intimacy

Objectives

By the power of the Holy Spirit working through God's Word, participants will (1) learn that biblical intimacy is that which is born of mutual commitment and service in the context of God's view of marriage, (2) affirm that the biblical view of marriage is that of an even deeper intimacy than mere physical partnership or mutual agreement, and (3) confess that only the forgiving love in Christ in the context of a committed married relationship can provide the place where true intimacy can thrive.

Opening Worship

Sing "Blest Be the Tie That Binds" (*LW* 295). The tie that binds is Christ's love experienced within a committed relationship that relies on His forgiveness. This tie must begin a couple's journey to emotional, spiritual, and physical intimacy that God desires for them in marriage. Open with prayer.

Focus

Ask someone to read the opening paragraph. Ask participants to comment on the discussion-starter question.

24. Answers will vary. A few years ago, Dr. Ruth Westheimer became popular by counseling people on intimacy and sex. Dr. Ruth claimed that we needed to quit being so repressed (often blamed on the Church) and be more open with our sexuality and intimacy. However, such a coarse approach, coupled with a mechanical or functional view of sexuality and intimacy, actually limits the intimacy that a person can share with another. The Bible's view of intimacy is something that is built over time with willful commitment. When emotional and sexual intimacy is expressed within a lifelong committed relationship, fear dissipates, apprehension is removed, and intimacy is shared in the context of trust and love.

Leave and Hold Fast (Inform)

25. Genesis portrays a man setting aside (leaving) familial ties and binding himself (holding fast) to his wife. This oneness is a gift that flows from the action of leaving and holding fast. The image is of something so intimately together that what was once two is now truly one. When Jesus quotes this passage from the Septuagint (the Greek Old Testament), He reiterates both the two-ness and the oneness, the great mystery of love in action within marriage.

26. "Leave" and "hold fast" speak of the refocusing of the man to the woman and the intimacy that is built when the women receives such a committed love. "Leave" demonstrates the necessary separation from other concerns, now placing the needs of one's spouse above all other relationships. "Hold fast" speaks of the ongoing connection of that love where the man focuses his energy and his work to loving his wife and, by extension, his family. The wife's reciprocation of that love willingly entrusts her happiness and joy to such a spouse. Intimacy is something that grows in an atmosphere of committed love. Committed love demonstrates itself by leaving, holding fast, and responding. Whenever there seems to be a problem in marriages, one needs to refer to these two actions: leaving and holding fast. If these are violated, the oneness and harmony in marriage that God desires is seriously compromised.

27. The marriage relationship, the context for a deep emotional, spiritual, and sexual intimacy, begins with commitment. "Leave" and "hold fast" are actions of the will, just like the marriage vows: the "I dos" or "I wills." In essence, both are promises to continually practice such love in the bonds of marriage.

28. "What therefore God has joined together" (v. 6) is an aspect of marriage from the beginning. In Matthew 19, the people challenging Jesus viewed marriage as a disposable partnership. Jesus not only corrects such a misunderstanding ("from the beginning it [divorce] was not so" [v. 8]), but He also teaches the depth of the intimacy lost when marriages are torn apart. His warning, "What therefore God has joined together, let not man separate," compels us to remember that while divorce is sometimes the lesser of two evils (when compared with adultery or abandonment), something very significant is lost. Those who take divorce lightly, almost practicing serial divorce, begin to scar the heart's capacity for intimacy, making that heart more and more callous.

29. The Bible can't get more down to earth and practical than this chapter. God's desire for man and wife is to be so certainly connected to Him by faith and so specifically directed to each other that even their bodies are completely at the disposal of the other. Such a physical availability for each other has to be rooted in more than our best intentions. It is rooted in God's sense of humanity both as the apex of His creation and as full recipients of His gracious mercy. When men's and women's identities are rooted in God's perspective of themselves, such confidence can begin to cause both men and women to submit themselves in loving service to another's needs.

30. The Bible again demonstrates itself as both a book of grace and a book of realism. It is true that marriage provides the occasion for intimacy, especially healthy sexual intimacy. But the Bible is very realistic about the depth of sin, its rebelliousness toward God and toward neighbor. It realizes that love is often lost in lust, that desire to have the other often trumps the desire to serve one another. Marriage, then, is an ideal to strive for as well as a relational remedy for men and women's inability to focus on the loving work that needs to be done for intimacy to thrive.

Loving Commitment (Connect)

31. Cohabitation destroys real intimacy by putting the actions of physical intimacy before lifelong commitment. It makes us physically and emotionally vulnerable to those who have yet to say, "I will love you," "I will learn to love you," and "I do." Nothing more destructive can happen to intimacy than to give oneself over and over again to those who by their actions are saying, "I love you only when you're worth it to me, only when you prove it to me."

32. Leaving father and mother and holding fast to one's spouse reorders one's relationships in their proper hierarchy. It's not that the extended family is unimportant or that other friendships are to be dispensed with. Rather, marriage requires that all relationships be ordered under the most important human relationship: the relationship to one's spouse. All other relationships are to be judged according to how they help us be the husband or the wife, the father or the mother, that God intends for us to be. Honoring our husband or loving our wife above all other earthly relationships and resisting the temptation to seek an intimacy elsewhere than in our marriage is God's way of keeping the bonds of marriage strong and intimacy intact.

Commitment Comes First (Vision)

33. Answers may vary. Romance may be the spark that ignites the flame of committed love, but committed love is the fuel that allows romance to be rekindled again and again. Romance is the joy of doing the little things that make our spouses feel loved and cared for. Romance is the upfront desire to love. Mature love is always open to the joys of romance rekindled again and again. In fact, all the little romantic things spouses do for one another are like the drops of glue that bond two objects together as one. Leaving/holding-fast love is always willing to start afresh, never taking the blessing of a loving spouse for granted.

34. The actions of intimacy in sexual intercourse do not merely solicit pleasure. The spiritual, emotional, and intimate oneness provided only through a pledge of lifelong fidelity should properly precede the physical intimacy of sexual intercourse. Paul's warning against being "joined to a prostitute" is that there is an intimacy there that can't be ignored (1 Corinthians 6:16). Such an intimacy debauched by lack of commitment and selfish desire for sexual pleasure apart from a commitment to one's spouse, or completely closed to the possibility of procreating new life, has ramifications for not only the body and spirit of the individual, but for the oneness of the marriage body as well. Lack of commitment attacks the oneness of the spirit-flesh unity of husband and wife. Immorality and adultery with another, or even self-centered sexual pleasure for oneself alone, militates against the oneness God desires to give people who seek His blessing of marriage.

Exercising Faith and Love

Objectives

By the power of the Holy Spirit working through God's Word, participants will (1) learn that according to the Bible marriage is a lifelong, joyous exercise of faith and love; (2) celebrate the Bible's distinctions of faith-filled, loving service for both husband (self-sacrificial love) and wife (submission); and (3) explore the value of male headship and female body-ship as a way to see the unique and mutually supporting blessings men and women bring to marriage.

Opening Worship

Sing "Oh, Blest the House, Whate'er Befall" (*TLH* 625). Marriage is the opportunity to put faith in Jesus to work in loving the one God created for us. Husband and wife commit to loving each other in all things by trusting in their forgiving Savior, Jesus Christ. Open with prayer.

Focus

Ask someone to read the opening paragraph out loud. Ask participants to comment on the discussion-starter question.

35. Answers may vary. The '60s tried to establish the human being as androgynous, as if men and women weren't truly unique. While our society may have begun to remedy inequalities between the sexes, at the same time it appears to have overlooked, diminished, or dismissed the unique gifts of male and female. The Bible encourages us to look at the unique and complementary differences created by our heavenly Father as opportunities to serve one another in love within marriage. Love is an exercise.

Mutual Submission, Submission, and Love (Inform)

36. The Bible emphasizes the mutual submission of believers who, under the inspiration of the Holy Spirit, serve one another in love.

Such submissions are acts of the will and commitments to love others as we ourselves were first loved by Christ (1 John 4:7–12, 19). In Christ, we are all "sons of God," "one in Christ," "Abraham's offspring," and "heirs according to promise" (Galatians 3:26–29). Nevertheless, our equality before God in Christ, and the mutual submission we owe to each other, does not destroy ordered social, relational, or sexual distinctions, but rather transcends them.

37. "Out of reverence for Christ" (Ephesians 5:21) is the key to understanding the inter-Christian relationships that have been redeemed and restored for the purposes that God intends. Such reverence sees Christ as the power source, the ultimate reference point in the relationship. In Christ, believers serve each other in love not simply out of respect for each other, but in full view of the gracious relationship they have received through Christ's atoning sacrifice and glorious resurrection. Freed from the power of sin through His blood, the Christian husband and wife exercise both love *and* faith. As we will see later, Christ liberates and enables both husband and wife to enjoy their created and ordered roles and responsibilities in faith-filled, loving service to one another.

38. Some see relationships, including marriages, as fifty-fifty propositions in which each person does his or her fair share. Experience proves that such expectations are unrealistic and that relationships based on such expectations will not last. The sustaining power for healthy gender roles and healthy marriages is God our Father, through faith in His Son, by the Spirit's power (see 1 Corinthians 11:11–12). When Christ becomes the reverence point of our loving service, we start asking questions such as "How may I love my neighbor?" At work that becomes "How may I serve my employer?" In marriage it is "How may I serve my wife?" or "How may I serve my husband?"

39. Paul transitions from speaking about the mutual submission believers owe one another in Christ (v. 21) to the submission a wife offers her husband (v. 22; see also Titus 2:4–5; 1 Peter 3:1–6), who is her "head", (v. 23; see also 1 Corinthians 11:3). The equality of man and wife before God in Christ is not lost in this submission, however. For his part, the husband is to model his service toward his wife ("love" [vv. 25, 28, 33]) based on Christ's exemplary service to the Church, which included giving up His own life. The extent of this loving service is even more than the wife is required to do. The wife is the husband's "body" (vv. 28–29; see also 1 Peter 3:7; Colossians

3:19), inferring that his own healthy existence depends upon his full, loving, caring support of her both spiritually and bodily.

40. Headship is frequently misunderstood as a "who's in charge and who gets to give the orders" proposition. That is not the way of Christian headship. The Greek word *kephale* is used here, and it doesn't mean the "status or position of leader." Rather, *kephale* is a field commander, the one who goes into battle first and who leads by example, even to the point of risking his own life (self-sacrificial love). Such headship entails being ultimately accountability for all whom one leads and serves. The husband and father is accountable to God for how his wife and children are loved, cared for, and served. There are both temporal (Proverbs 29:15; Colossians 3:21) and spiritual (1 Peter 3:7) consequences for husbands and fathers who do not fulfill their duties.

41. Headship and body-ship have different emphases, different ordered roles to play within the marriage. While the Scriptures indicate the created, redeemed, and sanctified equality of man and woman in God's eyes and according to original righteousness (the "image of God" in Genesis 1:27), the woman was created as "a helper fit for" the man (Genesis 1:18, 20). Without her, it is "not good" for him (2:18), but with her it is "very good" (1:31). In marriage, the wife has a God-created, God-blessed role to play as the recipient of the husband's self-sacrificial love. Proverbs 31:10–31 details the inexpressible value of a wife of noble character, one who fears the Lord (v. 30).

42. Marriage has a purpose. It satisfies body and soul, provides for mutual love and support, and, when and where God wills, results in the gift of children. More than that, in the Christian marriage, husband and wife point to the "mystery" of Christ and the Church (Ephesians 5:31–32). "Heirs with you of the grace of life" shows that in marriage God's grace and forgiveness in Christ are both given and received by husband and wife, who serve one another in love, enabled by God's love in Christ.

Love in Action (Connect)

43. Marriage is an exciting opportunity to exercise the many facets of love, which flow from faith. It is an adventure of seeing what is and what yet can be in one's marriage. Marriage encompasses the joy of knowing that the fires of romance may ignite at many different

times, but they burn most brightly in the actions of committed, loving service to each other, out of reverence for Christ.

44. Submission is an act of the will to serve another for Christ—a strength rather than a weakness. Submission means to commit oneself to serve just as Christ serves us, exercising God's unlimited love in Christ. Allow participants to discuss how we readily submit to the advice of our doctors, the direction of our employer, the instruction of our teacher, and to the laws of our government. Submission is simply part of an ordered existence and should not necessarily be construed negatively.

Learning to Love (Vision)

45. "Submitting to one another" (Ephesians 5:21) not only describes the "what" of our actions, but it also describes the "to whom": our neighbor. The focal point of reverence (Jesus) makes mutual submission happen. The promise of this passage is that God's love is at work in our relationships in such a way that we not only are dependent on Him, but we are bonded to each other as well. God, who loves us intimately in Christ, deepens our love for Him and for each other through His means of grace.

Our confidence, which comes from Christ, means that one's care for one's spouse is given freely (Matthew 10:8). In Christ, a husband's self-sacrificial love and a wife's submission to her husband reclaim the interpersonal relationship enjoyed by Adam and Eve in the Garden of Eden before it was lost through the fall into sin.

46. Attempts at self-actualization and renewed self-worth fruitlessly search for meaning through endless self-analyzing or narcissistic activities. In contrast, the Bible shows that blessings flow through faith in Christ and are extended through one's service to others. The marriage relationship of husband and wife is the place where such exercising of faith and love is highly blessed to the point of a man more fully realizing his masculinity and a woman her femininity within the context of that marriage. Knowing this surely helps us to become the man or the woman that God desires us to be.

More than Romance

Objectives

By the power of the Holy Spirit working through God's Word, participants will (1) learn the uniqueness that God's love in Christ brings to marriage, (2) affirm the importance of forgiveness in the marriage of two people who bring not only their hopes and dreams but also their sins into the marriage, and (3) rejoice that worship, the study of Scripture, and prayer are not addenda to marriage, but essential ingredients to a happy marriage in God's plan for men and women.

Opening Worship

Sing "Holy Father, in Your Mercy" (*LW* 469). God's love and mercy in Christ are the strength for marriage that is redeemed and restored for the purposes for which God created it. Marriage is meant as a blessing. God's merciful love in Christ enables marriage toward that end. Open with prayer.

Focus

Ask someone to read the opening paragraph. Ask participants to comment on the discussion-starter question.

47. Lead participants to see that marriage (a gift from God) is meant to create and sustain love. Love is not a feeling; above all it is a commitment, an act of will to serve another rather than oneself. This is the *agape* love that ultimately is God's alone. We can never manufacture such love disconnected from God. However, through faith in Christ, God does indeed share *agape* love with us, and we in turn share *agape* love with others. In the modern mind, where marriage is anything we want it to be and commitment is optional, one wonders if such a love can even be imagined anymore. It is telling that many today believe that long-term marriages are almost extinct, something that existed only in the past. Could past generations have seen such love as possible for all because they viewed marriage as necessary and sacred?

Christ and His Bride (Inform)

48. The marriage relationship is not merely for our individual happiness. It reflects something about God's love to us, just as God's love for the world—especially His Church—teaches us about the purpose of our love for each other. Obviously, the difference between our love and God's love is vast, even incomprehensibly distinct (the mystery of Christ's love for the Church [v. 32]). However, the Christian (one who receives God's love graciously given) does radiate and reflect the love of God to others. In this way, Christ's love for His bride, the Church, can be an example to men as to how to love their wives, and the Church's submission to its beloved Savior can be an example of how wives should submit to their husbands. The depth of Christ's love for the Church can never be reduced to mere example; it always remains the resource for such love in human relationships.

49. God's love radiates from Himself in care and service to others. *Agape* is the word that is used in these passages, and it is by definition "selfless love." (This love is not *philos*—brotherly love; *storge*—family love; or *eros*—sexual love.) In this regard, one could say that not only does God alone love this way, but God "IS" this love. Look more closely at 1 Corinthians 13 for other descriptions of this selfless love. The point to be made is that God wishes for His people to receive this love through faith in His Son and to share it with others.

Ecclesiastes 4 speaks of the value of true friendship and hints at the blessing of marriage (amidst disgust with the world). Throughout the passage, the author speaks about the blessing of another, but at the end he gives the picture of a "threefold cord" that is stronger still. This picture paints not only the value of a husband to his wife or a wife to her husband, but also to God's love in the midst of such a union.

50. The selfless love of God is vital to marriage. Not only are people unique in how they need to be loved, they also sinful and self-centered by nature (see again Genesis 3 and its depiction of the unraveling of human relationships). A constant temptation presents itself: to do what is in our own sinful self-interest. God's Word not only exposes that (the work of the Law in our lives, see Romans 3:19–20), but it also provides the Christ-earned declaration of forgiveness and mercy (2 Corinthians 5:17–20) that is needed to overcome these barriers to His love in our relationships with others.

51. God's merciful, forgiving love in Christ is not esoteric or otherworldly. It reaches down to the level where we live, the place full

of our failures and sins as well as our hopes and dreams. Romans 12 speaks about the priority of mercy in life. All of life is to be redemptively lived "by the mercies of God" (v. 1). Worship, study, and prayerful dialogue with God's Word literally find God bringing His love and mercy in Christ to the place we live. His mercy enables us to "present your bodies" (Romans 12:1) in service to others (to truly live again).

Mercy is wonderfully graphic when enfleshed in human nature. It doesn't remove one from the world; it redeems one to live godly lives in this world, with our families, friends, and neighbors. As living sacrifices, we are offered up and poured out, yet we are never extinguished like consumed sacrifices. Service to others in view of God's mercy never exhausts us like service motivated by guilt or greed.

The passage from 1 Corinthians wonderfully speaks about the redemption of life in human flesh. The passage speaks about the physical nature of love in the midst of the issues of prayer and mission. Paul reminds us that Christian teaching does not denigrate the human body. Spiritualistic teachings that overemphasize the human spirit at the expense of the human body or hedonistic teachings that dismiss the human spirit altogether miss the joy of the celebration of the physical level of life and love lived in the sphere of God's acclamation and direction.

52. Here Paul is dealing with a very real problem. All of 1 Corinthians 7 speaks about the concerns of family life and the pressing need of sharing the Gospel in the midst of persecution. Families are part of God's plan even in the midst of struggle. Paul speaks about prayer and one's relationship with God as vital to the bond of marriage and a source of joy even for the sexual aspect of love. While one's spiritual relationship with God always takes priority, it never denigrates the love that God wishes for us to express to each other. It elevates both, as this passage clearly teaches.

53. Colossians 3 is a description of the new life in Christ, which is given through faith in Him. The very gracious love of God certainly received is the source of strength to love and serve others. Paul specifically tells us about the "new clothes" that we wear: compassion, kindness, humility, meekness, and patience, forgiving as God in Christ forgave us. It is Christ's action for us that makes our actions for others possible. Paul then invites the Colossian Christians to "Let the word of Christ dwell in you richly" (v. 16), which produces a harvest of thanksgiving and thanks-living to those whom we love.

Christians believe that the hearing and receiving of God's love and forgiveness in Christ—in Word and Sacraments—is what we need in order to love as He has loved us. It is first and foremost God coming to us to forgive and bless us in Christ. Our songs, offerings, prayers, and lifestyle are responses to what He graciously gives to us through His Son.

The Power of Forgiveness (Connect)

54. The struggle in any meaningful relationship is the vulnerability of being transparent in the hands of another sinful person. Our temptation is to keep a record of wrongs, to be moved to anger because of someone's disregard for our thoughts and feelings. We hold on to our anger as a means of self-preservation and protection. In the minds and hearts of sinful people, these thoughts and feelings can burn in us as rage and revenge until they consume us. At this point, sin must be confronted by the justice of a God who never lets sin go unpunished and by the mercy of God in Christ who makes a fresh start truly possible. Paul reminds us that God was just in punishing His Son for our sins (in our stead) and merciful in granting His righteousness to us as a gift when he says, "Forgiving one another, as God in Christ forgave you." This reality makes putting away "bitterness and wrath" possible.

The Gospel, Baptism, Absolution, and the Lord's Supper are constant reminders of the cost of our forgiveness. These are the very means by which God delivers the forgiveness won by Christ to us. Hebrews 12:1–3 speaks about the joy that Christ had in suffering for His rebellious people because of their coming again to faith and life with God. This is the reality that the Christian returns to daily as he or she seeks to love the other.

55. Plans for marriage include issues concerning finances, home, children, and, then, the wedding. The most important aspect of a wedding—and a marriage—is the blessing and forgiveness of God and the presence and promise of Christ. Knowing these things will be vital when dealing with the tough challenges that life brings to marriage.

His Love Is Our Strength (Vision)

56. Only Christ's love can overcome our insecurities. Only Christ's love can give us confidence to serve when our feelings dictate

otherwise. Only Christ's love can help one see the impact of one's actions and the opportunities when seeking to love one's spouse as one is loved. Romance burns off of our emotions. For such emotion to rekindle itself over and over again, it must be fueled by the kind of love that cannot be extinguished. Such love is found in the actions of God in Christ, the stories of Christmas and Easter, delivered by His Word and His gifts to us.

57. "Grace alone" is a clear tenet of Scripture and of the Lutheran faith. One's relationship with God (and with others) can never be certain if it depends on the actions of sinful people. Thank God that He doesn't leave the world's need for His love dependent on our best actions (which amount to nothing before Him and fail time and time again toward one other). Our confidence before God comes from His action in Christ toward us. Our confidence in the resource of His love flows from His promise to bless us, to finish the job with us (Philippians 1:6). That confidence in God's Word, forgiveness, and mercy overflows from us into the lives of others. It is a confidence that doesn't depend on another's reaction to one's service (although love in return sure is nice!). It is the confidence, esteem, and strength for service that can only be described as "Christ in you, the hope of glory" (Colossians 1:27; see also 1 Corinthians 6:17–19).

Leaving a Legacy

Objectives

By the power of the Holy Spirit working through God's Word, participants will (1) learn that marital love is naturally to be extended beyond the love of one's spouse, (2) give thanks that children are that natural extension of married love and a part of God's plan for marital blessing, and (3) affirm that healthy marriages are foundational to a healthy society from the Bible's perspective.

Opening Worship

Sing "Lord, While for Humankind We Pray" (*LW* 502). God's plan is for strong marriages to be a blessing to society to help build strong communities. Notice how the hymn bids us to sing for blessing beyond our own personal concerns. Open with prayer.

Focus

Why don't we hear commercials like this? (Take off on the MasterCard commercial) The cost of piano lessons, school, uniforms and jerseys, the costs of dances, and of course the late nights worrying as they get older. . . . But, the joy of raising a child and watching him or her become the man or woman that God means for him or her to be . . . priceless!

58. The value of healthy families to society cannot be overestimated. Each God-given role—father, mother, child—is important. Healthy marriages provide for healthy families; well-cared-for and much-loved children grow to be productive citizens. Healthy families are blessings to the community, which in turn should support the family as an institution.

Doing Your Duty (Inform)

59. The family is the primary place where faith and values are transmitted. Ultimately, the teaching of God's Word is the most

essential duty of parents, especially fathers (v. 7). The goal of such work is the raising up of a family in the faith. As Deuteronomy 6:2 says, this matter is about life itself.

60. Proverbs teaches us that such training will aid our children when they too must face life as adults. The purpose of teaching God's Word to children is to prepare our children for life—life lived with God by faith, in worship and study of Him, and in care and support for those we love (work and family). To fail to prepare a child for the opportunity of becoming a godly adult is to fail at what is most basic in God's expectations of parents.

61. Matthew 23:37 and Hebrews 12:6–10 speak about how mother and father might fulfill such duties as God's representatives to their children. Our world senses some value in maternal love, the unconditional love of mothers, but one needs to understand that the disciplinary love of fathers is also vital to a child's maturation. The long-suffering love of a mother may be different than the setting-boundaries love of a disciplining father, but each has its godly purpose.

Parental instincts must also be aligned to the Word of God as to the teaching and moral direction necessary in raising children. Titus 2:1–5 reveals that men and women must constantly be encouraged to strive for what is godly in our love for each other. We are aware of our constant tendency as sinful people to do the opposite. Doing merely what comes naturally is to open oneself up to the dangers of one aspect of love—the maternal danger of becoming too attached or the paternal danger of becoming too detached—dominating to the exclusion of the other. Here parents learn to balance each other in the work of godly parenting according to God's lead in the Scripture and for the child's good.

62. Children are a blessing to families, a gift of God. Like in the ancient world, children today sometimes are not valued because they produce nothing society values yet cost much. Jesus demonstrates children's value as God's gifts by calling them to Himself amidst the rebukes to the contrary from His own disciples.

Children are God's blessing to marriages in that both father and mother will have to devote their energies into the love and guiding of another. Child rearing gives us a very practical glimpse of how God Himself loves us. While children are sinful and selfish from birth, and, indeed, from conception (Psalm 51:5), there is also a simple trust and a joy that children exude, especially when they know they are loved.

Such joy is a reflection of our relationship to God as our heavenly Father.

63. Abortion on demand is the final expression of that idea that children are addendums to our lifestyle on our terms alone. This mentality sees children as having to fit our life expectations and life goals. Conversely, a mind-set that sees children as God's gifts who come into our lives to raise us to maturity (as we do them) in God's love and joy sees that our lives (jobs, time, talents, etc.) are to be used for the sake of our spouse and children. In the Bible's view, nothing is more vital or precious in this world than our spouse and children.

64. The Fourth Commandment demonstrates clearly the Bible's value of family: father, mother, and child. The State does not tower over the family but is derived from the authority of parents (Large Catechism I 141). In this sense, the State is called to serve the goals of the family by maintaining peace and order. In such an environment, the family is able to work and grow.

Children develop a healthy respect for all authority as they learn to honor their parents. Honoring one's parents is God's way of building a climate of respectfulness out of which love can grow and be sustained. As the family learns its rightful, joyous place before God the Father, and children learn their place before their parents, a healthy view of civic authority extends. Even with "faulty" parents, one can learn to disagree without disrespect. This lesson learned blesses a community as well.

65. Adultery destabilizes marriages. Serial divorce creates the mind-set that there is no permanence in love, solidifying the destructive expectation that breakup and loss are the norm in life. Such an expectation not only leaves husbands and wives looking to fend for themselves, but it also leaves children broken and without guidance. Jesus warns in Matthew 19:6, "What therefore God has joined together, let not man separate." Interestingly, Matthew records Jesus' love for the children right after this section about the abuse of divorce.

Marriages need an environment of commitment for true intimacy to grow, but families also need that same environment to raise children, to give them time to know and practice the difference between love and lust, between right and wrong, good and bad, selflessness and selfishness. When a community has to do what the family will not, when it is clamoring for government to enforce good behavior, the Church says, "Look first at the families, rebuild there!"

66. 1 Peter 2 clearly shows an order of respect: "Be subject for the Lord's sake to all authority" and "Love the brotherhood. Fear God. Honor the emperor." Governmental authority derives itself from the institutions that God has laid as foundational, namely the authority of mother and father (see the Fourth Commandment). A modern myth suggests that government can step in and replace many duties of the father and the mother. The Bible warns against such a view. Parental responsibility cannot be replaced by programs or policies. There are times when certain parents abdicate their responsibility and society must step in for the sake of the child. It is in the community's best interest to strengthen our parents for their tasks, challenging them and assisting them to fulfill their responsibilities to their families.

Mother and Father (Connect)

67. Discuss these questions with care and sensitivity—not everyone grows up in a two-parent household, and not everyone will raise children with both mother and father in the home. The teamwork of parenting, learning to work together to raise up children as blessings from God, concretely demonstrates the many facets of God's love to a child. There are many examples of a mother's strength, a father's perseverance, and so on.

68. Christian families want to be integral parts of their community because God's love always extends outward to others. The temptation today is for many communities to isolate themselves from one another and to love what they like, either out of selfishness or fear. This kind of love stunts the growth of the Christian and the Christian family. Families learn to love by committing themselves to one another, even as they are unique and distinct. Such love is to be extended out from the family to one's neighbors, those like us and those not (for example, see Luke 10, the parable of the Good Samaritan, and Acts 10). God calls us to love that which is unlike us, since that remains the essence of His love for us. The family may be a place of security and growth, the church may be that as an extended family of faith, but such blessings are always meant to strengthen God's people to reach beyond their zones of comfort to exercise God's love in the power of faith. The post-Communion prayer says it best, "In faith toward You and in fervent love toward one another" (*Lutheran Worship*).

Community Blessings (Vision)

God's whole effort to redeem and restore His creation started with a promise (Genesis 3:15), but very soon it was rooted in a family, a bloodline, Abraham's family (Genesis 12:1–3). This family was the place where God firmly established His love in human history so that the whole world might know Him through Abraham's Seed, Jesus Christ.

69. Caring for our spouse and our children not only matures us, it also helps us to rely on God and His Word in very real-world ways. Such wisdom surely extends outward from one's family to one's community. While families not only strive for right actions of husbands, wives, and children, but also for right motivations, learning the value of such things helps one discern the value of civic outward good works as well.

70. It is too easy to think that the family can be replaced by the functions it provides. Resources, nurture, education, and guidance can come from someplace else, but these serve to support the family, not to replace it. The relationship of father, mother, and child is so intimate that each person sees the other as an extension of self. Rather than seeking to dismiss or replace the family, communities do well to nurture and support the family's ability to care for one another. If mutual responsibility and care does not exist in the family, they cannot exist elsewhere for long.

Glossary

abortion. Any deliberate act to terminate a pregnancy by destroying human life. In 1973, abortion (within certain parameters) was legalized in all states by the U.S. Supreme Court (*Roe v. Wade*).

abortifacient. Any substance that induces an abortion. RU-486 (Mifepristone) is probably the most controversial abortifacient. A possible side effect of "the pill" is that, in addition to prohibiting pregnancy, it may also act as an abortifacient.

adultery. Generally defined, adultery is consensual sexual intercourse by a married person with someone other than his or her legal spouse. However, all sexual activity outside of heterosexual marriage falls under the condemnation of the Sixth Commandment: "You shall not commit adultery" (Exodus 20:14).

annulment. A legal declaration that a marriage is null and void.

antinomianism. The belief that Christians are free from many, if not all, of the constraints of moral law.

civil union. A civil status similar to marriage that allows same-sex persons (and, in some states and nations, opposite-sex couples) access to benefits traditionally reserved for heterosexual married couples.

contraception. Any action, device, or medication used to prevent a woman from becoming pregnant. Some contraceptives are prescribed to alleviate specific conditions or to regulate menstruation. Prior to the 1930 Lambeth Conference of Anglican bishops, most Protestant churches (including Lutheran) condemned contraception. In 1965, the U.S. Supreme Court struck down a state law prohibiting contraception for heterosexual married couples (*Griswold v. Connecticut*), virtually legalizing contraception for this country.

divorce. Dissolution of marriage or the ending of marriage before the death of either spouse.

evangelical. Literally, "good news"—the Gospel. This term is often used to describe churches that stress the Gospel of Jesus Christ in their teachings, especially His death and resurrection to save people from their sin and grant them eternal life.

fornication. Generally defined as sexual activity between two unmarried persons.

Gospel. The message of Christ's death and resurrection for the forgiveness of sins and eternal life. The Holy Spirit works through the Gospel to create and sustain faith and to empower good works. The Gospel is found in both the Old and New Testaments.

justification. God declares sinners to be just or righteous for Christ's sake; that is, God has imputed or charged our sins to Christ and He imputes or credits Christ's righteousness to us.

Law. God's will that shows people how they should live (e.g., the Ten Commandments) and condemns their failure. The preaching of the Law is the cause of contrition, or genuine sorrow over sin. The Law is found in both the Old and New Testaments.

marriage. Historically, a publicly recognized, lifelong relationship of two opposite-sex individuals who are not too closely related for the purpose of mutual support, sexual intimacy, and the bearing and nurture of children. Jesus affirmed the biblical basis for traditional marriage, the lifelong one-flesh union of husband and wife (Matthew 19:4–6).

polemical. From the Greek word for "battle." The term describes conversation or writing that attacks and refutes.

sanctification. The spiritual growth that follows justification by grace through faith in Christ.